PAMPHLETS ON AMERICAN WRITERS · NUMBER 21

UNIVERSITY OF MINNESOTA

Nathanael West

BY STANLEY EDGAR HYMAN

UNIVERSITY OF MINNESOTA PRESS · MINNEAPOLIS

Printed in the United States of America at
the Jones Press, Inc., Minneapolis

Library of Congress Catalog Card Number: 62-63699

ISBN 0-8166-0278-6

second printing, 1971

PUBLISHED IN GREAT BRITAIN, INDIA, AND PAKISTAN BY THE OXFORD
UNIVERSITY PRESS, LONDON, BOMBAY, AND KARACHI, AND IN
CANADA BY THOMAS ALLEN, LTD., TORONTO

TO THE MEMORY OF LEONARD BROWN

Stanley Edgar Hyman was a staff writer for the *New Yorker* and book critic of the *New Leader* as well as a member of the literature faculty at Bennington College. Among his books are *The Tangled Bank, Poetry and Criticism,* and *The Armed Vision.*

↗Nathanael West

Nathanael West was born Nathan Weinstein in New York City on October 17, 1903, the child of Jewish immigrants from Russia. His mother, Anna Wallenstein Weinstein, came of a cultivated family, and had been a beautiful girl, courted in Europe by the painter Maurice Stern. As a housewife she turned stout and bossy. West's father, Max Weinstein, a building contractor, was slight, kind, and shy. Of West's two sisters, the elder, Hinda, somewhat resembled the mother, and the younger, Lorraine (called Laura), was more like the father. West was particularly devoted to his father, and so close to his younger sister that in later life he repeatedly said he could never marry less fine a woman than his sister Laura.

The boy West attended P.S. 81 and P.S. 10, both in Manhattan, where he showed no academic distinction. He was a thin, awkward, and ungainly child. Summers he went to Camp Paradox in the Adirondacks, and a former counselor remembers him as "a quiet chap and not much of a mixer." Baseball was his passion, although he tended to daydream in the outfield. When a fly ball hit him on the head and bounced off for a home run, he got the nickname, "Pep," that stayed with him all his life.

Otherwise West seems to have spent most of his time reading. If his sisters' recollection can be trusted, he read Tolstoi at ten, and by thirteen he was familiar with Dostoevski and other Russian literature, Flaubert, and Henry James. He trained his bull terrier to bite anyone who came into his room when he was reading. After his graduation from P.S. 10, West enrolled at De Witt Clinton High School, where he soon distinguished himself as one

5

of the weakest students in the school. He took no part in any extracurricular activity. In June 1920, West left Clinton without graduating.

In September 1921, West was admitted to Tufts University, on the strength of what now seems to have been a forged transcript from De Witt Clinton. Two months later, as a result of academic difficulties, he withdrew. In February 1922, he was admitted to Brown University as a transfer student from Tufts, this time on the basis of the transcript of the record of another Nathan Weinstein at Tufts. Once enrolled at Brown, West got serious, and managed not only to pass his courses but to graduate in two and a half years.

At Brown, West developed another personality, or showed another side of his personality than the solitary dreamer. He became an Ivy League fashion plate, wearing Brooks Brothers suits and shirts, and a homburg. A college friend, Jeremiah Mahoney, recalls that West looked like a "well-heeled mortuary assistant." Although his manner was reserved, he was friendly and gregarious, generous with his large allowance from his father, and a fairly good banjo player. With girls, he tended to be either too shy or too brash. One summer, West and another college friend, Quentin Reynolds, worked as hod carriers for West's father, and West not only built muscles on his thin frame but got on surprisingly well with the workmen.

West received little or no education in the Jewish religion, and although he was probably ritually circumcised, he was never confirmed in a Bar Mitzvah ceremony. During his years at Brown, West threw off what he could of his Jewishness, and suffered from the rest. "More than anyone I ever knew," his friend John Sanford later reported, "Pep writhed under the accidental curse of his religion." West had nothing to do with any organized Jewish activity on campus, hung around the snobbish Gentile fraternities, and was intensely anxious to be pledged and intensely bitter that he never was. "Nobody ever thought of Pep as being Jewish," a college friend has said, but apparently the Brown fraternities did. West's great success at Brown was as an aesthete. He dabbled in mysticism, ritual magic, and medieval Catholicism, quoted from obscure saints, discovered Joyce, and for a while was a Nietzschean. S. J. Perelman, a college friend who later married West's sister Laura, recalls that West was the first man on campus to read *Jurgen*. He was equally devoted to Baudelaire, Verlaine, and Rimbaud, Huysmans and Arthur Machen. His personal library was the largest any Brown man had at the time, and he loaned books liberally. Relying on the other Nathan Weinstein's credits in science and economics, West was able to confine himself almost entirely to courses in literature, philosophy, and history. His principal extracurricular activity was working as an editor of *Casements*, the Brown literary magazine. He drew its first cover design, naturally of casements, and contributed a poem, "Death," and an article, "Euripides — a Playwright." The 1924 *Liber Brunensis*, the yearbook, identified West as a genius with an unpredictable future.

After his graduation in 1924, West persuaded his father to send him to Paris, where he spent two happy years and grew a red beard. He returned to New York early in 1926, worked for his father for a while, and then in 1927, through a family connection, got a job as assistant manager at the Kenmore Hotel on East 23rd Street. Put on night duty, he was able to spend the nights reading. He gave rooms to his Brown friends and *their* homeless friends, among them Dashiell Hammett, who finished *The Maltese Falcon* as West's bootleg guest at the Kenmore. In 1928 he progressed to the same job at a fancier hotel, the Sutton on East 56th Street, where he put up other indigent writers, at reduced rates or no

7

charge at all, among them Erskine Caldwell and James T. Farrell. After the stock market crash, which ruined West's father, the Sutton's sun deck became a favored spot for suicides, and West took to calling it "Suicide Leap."

West's first novel, *The Dream Life of Balso Snell*, seems to have been first written in college, but he rewrote it at the Sutton, and in 1931 he managed to get it privately printed in a limited edition of 500 copies. One review appeared, in *Contempo*, but otherwise *Balso Snell* caused no stir whatsoever. The book listed "Nathanael West" as author and thus marked West's official change of name. He had spent much of his class time at Brown doodling "Nathan von Wallenstein Weinstein," which was the name signed to his *Casements* contributions, but even that had turned out to be not Gentile enough. West explained to William Carlos Williams how he got the name: "Horace Greeley said, 'Go West, young man.' So I did." West's anti-Semitism was now considerable. He referred to Jewish girls as "bagels," and avoided them.

In 1931, West took a leave from the Sutton and he and Sanford, another aspiring novelist, rented a shack in the Adirondacks near Warrensburg, New York. Here they wrote in the mornings and fished and hunted in the afternoons. West was working on *Miss Lonelyhearts*, reading each sentence back aloud, producing about a hundred words a day. He rewrote the manuscript five or six times, in the Adirondacks, then back at the Sutton; finally, having quit the Sutton, in a hotel in Frenchtown, New Jersey.

Late in 1932 West and the Perelmans bought a farmhouse in Bucks County, Pennsylvania, and Mrs. Weinstein soon moved in to take over the cooking and try to persuade West to return to the hotel business. In 1933 *Miss Lonelyhearts* was published, and it was reviewed enthusiastically. Unfortunately, the publisher, Horace Liveright, chose that moment to go bankrupt, the printer refused to deliver most of the edition, and by the time West got another publisher to take it over, the reviews were forgotten. Altogether *Miss Lonelyhearts* sold fewer than 800 copies, and West's total income from his first two books and three years of writing came to $780.

In 1932 West had become co-editor with Dr. Williams of a little magazine, *Contact*, and he published articles and chapters of *Miss Lonelyhearts* in it and in *Contempo* in 1933. In August 1933, he became associate editor of a magazine, *Americana*, edited by Alexander King. Before *Americana* expired in November, West managed to publish a Hollywood story, "Business Deal," and some excerpts from *Balso Snell* in it. West then wrote some stories for the slick magazines, but did not succeed in selling any. He applied for a Guggenheim fellowship, with F. Scott Fitzgerald as one of his sponsors, but failed to get it.

West next wrote *A Cool Million* in a hurry, hoping to profit from the reviews of *Miss Lonelyhearts* and make some money. It appeared in 1934, was unfavorably reviewed, sold poorly, and was soon remaindered.

West's personal life in the East was no more successful than his literary career. *Balso Snell* was dedicated to Alice Shepard, a Roman Catholic girl who had gone to Pembroke College with West's sister Laura. He was secretly engaged to her from 1929 to 1932, then publicly engaged, but they never married, although West had bought a marriage license and carried it around with him for several years. His poverty was the explanation given out, but in Sanford's opinion the engagement foundered on the religious difference.

West had been to Hollywood for a few months in 1933, when *Miss Lonelyhearts* was sold to Twentieth Century-Fox and West received a writing contract at $350 a week. He was given little to do, saw his novel made into a Lee Tracy murder thriller, and came back to New York in July disillusioned and bitter. Nevertheless, in 1935, when every other possibility seemed closed to him, West returned to Hollywood and went to work for Republic Studios as a script writer. He switched to RKO Radio in 1938, and also worked for Universal-International Pictures. In the remaining few years of his life, West turned out a number of trivial screenplays, alone or in collaboration, among them *Five Came Back, I Stole a Million,* and *Spirit of Culver.* As a result of his facility as a script writer, West was able to live in comfort and security for the first time since the 1929 crash. He worked a few hours a week dictating to a secretary, and spent most of his weekends on hunting trips, following the season down from Oregon through California into Mexico each year. He acquired two hunting dogs, which slept on his bed, and he explained to people that he needed a house and servants for the dogs.

West made it clear that he despised the "pants pressers" of Hollywood, and he tried to escape in a number of fashions. He collaborated on two plays for Broadway, but the first never got there and the second only lasted two performances, winning from Brooks Atkinson the accolade "nitwit theatre." He became a fellow traveler of the Communist party, signing the call for the American Writers Congress in 1935, joining the Screen Writers Guild, and working strenuously on behalf of Loyalist Spain and other causes. (Earlier, in 1933, he had published a Marxist poem in *Contempo.* Before leaving for California in 1935 he had picketed Orbach's with other Communist sympathizers and was jailed for a few hours "for obstructing traffic.") He was, luckily, unable to get his political orientation explicitly into his fiction.

West published *The Day of the Locust* in 1939, hoping its success would get him out of Hollywood, but despite some good reviews it was a commercial failure, selling fewer than 1500 copies. (West's publisher, Bennett Cerf, explained to him that it failed because women readers didn't like it.)

West's isolation ended suddenly and surprisingly in 1940, when he fell in love with Eileen McKenney, the protagonist of Ruth McKenney's *My Sister Eileen*. They were married in April, and spent a three-month honeymoon in Oregon, hunting and fishing. On West's return he got a higher paid job at Columbia Pictures; later Columbia bought *A Cool Million* and a screen treatment of it on which West had collaborated. The great happy period of West's life, begun in the spring, did not last out the year. On December 22, the Wests were returning from a hunting trip in Mexico, when West, a poor driver, went through a stop sign near El Centro, California. Their station wagon crashed into an automobile. Eileen died instantly, West an hour later on the way to the hospital. He was thirty-seven. His body was shipped to New York and buried in a Jewish cemetery.

Since his death West's reputation has risen continuously. *Miss Lonelyhearts* has sold 190,000 copies in paperback, and *The Day of the Locust* 250,000. Scholarly articles about West, here and abroad, multiply cancerously. *Miss Lonelyhearts* has been made into a play, a more faithful film than the Lee Tracy one, and an opera. In 1946 it was translated into French by Marcelle Sibon as *Mademoiselle Cœur-Brisé*, with an introduction by Philippe Soupault, and it has had a visible effect on later French fiction. Since 1949, all West's books but the first have been published in England. When the four novels were reissued in this country in one volume in 1957, all the reviews were favorable, and there was general agreement that West was one of the most important writers of the thirties, as American as apple pie. West's picture appeared on the cover of the *Saturday Review*, looking very Jewish.

The Dream Life of Balso Snell (1931) is almost impossible to synopsize. A poet named Balso Snell finds the wooden Trojan Horse and has a picaresque journey up its alimentary canal. In the course of his travels he encounters: a Jewish guide; Maloney the Areopagite, a Catholic mystic; John Gilson, a precocious schoolboy; and Miss McGeeney, John's eighth-grade teacher. Each has a story, sometimes several stories, to tell, and their stories merge with their dreams and with Balso's dreams in a thoroughly confusing, and deliberately confusing, fashion. The book ends with Balso's orgasm, still in the bowels of the horse, during a dream of rapturous sexual intercourse with Miss McGeeney. Balso is dreaming the schoolboy's dream, and may have become the schoolboy.

The overwhelming impression the reader gets is of the corruption and repulsiveness of the flesh. In one of John Gilson's fantasies of beating a mistress, he explains his action: "I have a sty on my eye, a cold sore on my lip, a pimple where the edge of my collar touches my neck, another pimple in the corner of my mouth, and a drop of salt snot on the end of my nose." Furthermore, "It seems to me as though all the materials of life — wood, glass, wool, skin — are rubbing against my sty, my cold sore and my pimples." When Balso encounters Miss McGeeney, a middle-aged tweedy woman disguised for the moment as a beautiful naked young girl, she offers him her poetic vision: "Houses that are protuberances on the skin of streets — warts, tumors, pimples, corns, nipples, sebaceous cysts, hard and soft chancres."

In a dream within his dream, Balso is attracted to girl cripples: "He likened their disarranged hips, their short legs, their humps, their splay feet, their wall-eyes, to ornament." He cries tenderly to one of them, Janey the hunchback: "For me, your sores are like flowers: the new, pink, budlike sores, the full, rose-ripe sores, the sweet, seed-bearing sores. I shall cherish them all." One of Balso's beautiful memories in the book is of a girl he once loved who did nothing all day but put bits of meat and gravy, butter and cheese, on the petals of roses so that they would attract flies instead of butterflies and bees.

As the human body is seen as a running sore, Christianity is seen entirely in terms of Christ's wounded and bleeding body. Maloney the Areopagite is writing a hagiography of Saint Puce, a flea who was born, lived, and died in the armpit of Jesus Christ. Maloney's blasphemous idea that Saint Puce was born of the Holy Ghost enables West to mock the mysteries of Incarnation, as the flea's feasting on the divine flesh and blood enables West to mock Eucharist. The Passion is burlesqued by Maloney, who is encountered naked except for a derby stuck full of thorns, trying to crucify himself with thumbtacks, and by Beagle Darwin, a fictional invention of Miss McGeeney's, who does a juggling act, keeping in the air "the Nails, the Scourge, the Thorns, and a piece of the True Cross."

Nor is West's bitterness in the book reserved for Christianity. Judaism comes in for its share. The song in praise of obscene roundness that Balso makes when he starts his journey concludes:

> Round and Ringing Full
> As the Mouth of a Brimming Goblet
> The Rust-Laden Holes
> In Our Lord's Feet
> Entertain the Jew-Driven Nails.

The guide turns out to be not only a Jew, but a Jew who at the mention of such melodious Jewish names as Hernia Hornstein and Paresis Pearlberg finds it necessary to affirm: "I am a Jew. I'm a Jew! A Jew!" Balso answers politely that some of his best friends are Jews, and adds Doughty's epigram: "The semites are like to a man sitting in a cloaca to the eyes, and whose brows touch heaven."

The strength of *Balso Snell* lies in its garish comic imagination. Maloney's crucifixion with thumbtacks is not only a serious theme that West's later work develops, it is also funny, and as a parody of the stance of Roman Catholic mysticism, devastating. The account in John Gilson's journal of his Gidean and Dostoevskian murder of an idiot dishwasher is repulsive but genuinely imagined, and its unconscious sexual motivation is boldly dramatized: stripping for the crime, John notices his genitals tight and hard; afterwards he feels like a happy young girl, "kittenish, cuney-cutey, darlingey, springtimey"; when he sees sailors on the street, he flirts and camps and feels "as though I were melting — all silk and perfumed, pink lace." The hunchback Janey is a nightmarish vision of the female body as terrifying, transformed into comedy: she has a hundred and forty-four exquisite teeth, and is pregnant in the hump.

Some of West's language in the book foreshadows his later triumphs. Janey imagines death to be "like putting on a wet [bathing] suit — shivery." John describes his dual nature to his fantasy-mistress, Saniette: "Think of two men — myself and the chauffeur within me. This chauffeur is very large and dressed in ugly ready-made clothing. His shoes, soiled from walking about the streets of a great city, are covered with animal ordure and chewing gum. His hands are covered with coarse woollen gloves. On his head is a derby hat." Sometimes John speaks in a voice we can hear as the youthful West's. He tells Balso: "I need women and because I can't buy or force them, I have to make poems for them. God knows how tired I am of using the insanity of Van Gogh and the adventures of Gauguin as can-openers." John explains his position in a pamphlet, which he sells to Balso for a dollar. In it he confesses: "If it had been possible for me to attract by exhibiting a series of physical charms, my hatred would have been less. But I found it necessary to substitute strange conceits, wise and witty sayings, peculiar conduct, Art, for the muscles, teeth, hair, of my rivals."

The weaknesses of *Balso Snell* are all characteristically juvenile. The principal one is the obsessive scatology, which soon becomes boring. "O Anus Mirabilis!" Balso cries of his rectal entrance to the Trojan Horse, and his roundness song takes off from that anal image. "Art is a sublime excrement," he is told by the Jewish guide (who seems to justify only the first half of Doughty's aphorism). John sees journal-keepers in excremental imagery: "They come to the paper with a constipation of ideas — eager, impatient. The white paper acts as a laxative. A diarrhoea of words is the result." When the idiot dishwasher swallows, John compares it to "a miniature toilet being flushed." As John beats Saniette, he cries: "O constipation of desire! O diarrhoea of love!" He has visions of writing a play that will conclude when "the ceiling of the theatre will be made to open and cover the occupants with tons of loose excrement." Balso speaks "with lips torn angry in laying duck's eggs from a chicken's rectum." James F. Light reports that West was fond of quoting Odo of Cluny's reference to the female as *"saccus stercoris,"* but the book's scatological obsession is clearly not restricted to the female. It is no less than a vision of the whole world as one vast dungheap.

Balso Snell is complex and stratified, so much so that at one point we get Janey's thinking as Beagle imagines it in a letter actually written by Miss McGeeney and read by Balso in his dream within a dream. But the book has no form, and consists merely of a series of encounters and complications, terminated rather than resolved by the orgasm. We can sense West's dissatisfaction with it as not fully realized in his re-use of some of its material in later works. Some of *Balso Snell* is extremely schoolboyish, like the guide's aphorism, "A hand in the Bush is worth two in the pocket," or Balso's comment on Maloney's story of the martyrdom and death of Saint Puce: "I think you're morbid. . . . Take cold showers."

When *Miss Lonelyhearts* was published two years later, in 1933, West told A. J. Liebling that it was entirely unlike *Balso Snell*, "of quite a different make, wholesome, clean, holy, slightly mystic and inane." He describes it in "Some Notes on Miss Lonelyhearts" as a "portrait of a priest of our time who has had a religious experience." In it, West explains, "violent images are used to illustrate commonplace events. Violent acts are left almost bald." He credits William James's *Varieties of Religious Experience* for its psychology. Some or all of this may be Westian leg-pull.

The plot of *Miss Lonelyhearts* is Sophoclean irony, as simple and inevitable as the plot of *Balso Snell* is random and whimsical. A young newspaperman who writes the agony column of his paper as "Miss Lonelyhearts" has reached the point where the joke has gone sour. He becomes obsessed with the real misery of his correspondents, illuminated for him by the cynicism of William Shrike, the feature editor. Miss Lonelyhearts pursues Shrike's wife Mary, unsuccessfully, and cannot content himself with the love and radiant goodness of Betty, his fiancée. Eventually he finds his fate in two of his correspondents, the crippled Peter Doyle and his wife Fay. Miss Lonelyhearts is not punished for his tumble with Fay, but when on his next encounter he fights her off, it leads to his being shot by Doyle.

The characters are allegorical figures who are at the same time convincing as people. Miss Lonelyhearts is a New England puritan, the son of a Baptist minister. He has a true religious vocation or calling, but no institutional church to embody it. When Betty suggests that he quit the column, he tells her: "I can't quit. And even if I were to quit, it wouldn't make any difference. I wouldn't be able to forget the letters, no matter what I did."

In one of the most brilliant strokes in the book, he is never named, always identified only by his role. (In an earlier draft,

West had named him Thomas Matlock, which we could translate "Doubter Wrestler," but no name at all is infinitely more effective.) Even when he telephones Fay Doyle for an assignation, he identifies himself only as "Miss Lonelyhearts, the man who does the column." In his namelessness, in his vocation without a church, Miss Lonelyhearts is clearly the prophet in the reluctance stage, when he denies the call and tells God that he stammers, but Miss Lonelyhearts, the prophet of *our* time, is stuck there until death.

Miss Lonelyhearts identifies Betty as the principle of order: "She had often made him feel that when she straightened his tie, she straightened much more." The order that she represents is the innocent order of Nature, as opposed to the disorder of sinful Man. When Miss Lonelyhearts is sick, Betty comes to nourish him with hot soup, impose order on his room, and redeem him with a pastoral vision: "She told him about her childhood on a farm and of her love for animals, about country sounds and country smells and of how fresh and clean everything in the country is. She said that he ought to live there and that if he did, he would find that all his troubles were city troubles." When Miss Lonelyhearts is back on his feet, Betty takes him for a walk in the zoo, and he is "amused by her evident belief in the curative power of animals." Then she takes him to live in the country for a few days, in the book's great idyllic scene. Miss Lonelyhearts is beyond such help, but it is Betty's patient innocence — she is as soft and helpless as a kitten — that makes the book so heartbreaking. She is an innocent Eve to his fallen Adam, and he alone is driven out of Eden.

The book's four other principal characters are savage caricatures, in the root sense of "caricature" as the overloading of one attribute. Shrike is a dissociated half of Miss Lonelyhearts, his cynical intelligence, and it is interesting to learn that Shrike's rhetorical masterpiece, the great speech on the varieties of escape, was spoken by Miss Lonelyhearts in an earlier draft. Shrike's name is marvelously apt. The shrike or butcherbird impales its prey on thorns, and the name is a form of the word "shriek." Shrike is of course the mocker who hands Miss Lonelyhearts his crown of thorns, and throughout the book he is a shrieking bird of prey; when not a butcherbird, "a screaming, clumsy gull."

Shrike's wife Mary is one vast teasing mammary image. As Miss Lonelyhearts decides to telephone Mary in Delehanty's speakeasy, he sees a White Rock poster and observes that "the artist had taken a great deal of care in drawing her breasts and their nipples stuck out like tiny red hats." He then thinks of "the play Mary made with her breasts. She used them as the coquettes of long ago had used their fans. One of her tricks was to wear a medal low down on her chest. Whenever he asked to see it, instead of drawing it out she leaned over for him to look. Although he had often asked to see the medal, he had not yet found out what it represented." Miss Lonelyhearts and Mary go out for a gay evening, and Mary flaunts her breasts while talking of her mother's terrible death from cancer of the breast. He finally gets to see the medal, which reads "Awarded by the Boston Latin School for first place in the 100 yd. dash." When he takes her home he kisses her breasts, for the first time briefly slowing down her dash.

The Doyles are presented in inhuman or subhuman imagery. When, in answer to Fay's letter of sexual invitation, Miss Lonelyhearts decides to telephone her, he pictures her as "a tent, hair-covered and veined," and himself as a skeleton: "When he made the skeleton enter the flesh tent, it flowered at every joint." Fay appears and is a giant: "legs like Indian clubs, breasts like balloons and a brow like a pigeon." When he takes her arm, "It felt like a thigh." Following her up the stairs to his apartment, "he watched the action of her massive hams; they were like two enormous grindstones." Undressing, "she made sea sounds; something flapped like a sail; there was the creak of ropes; then he heard the wave-against-a-wharf smack of rubber on flesh. Her call for him to hurry was a sea-moan, and when he lay beside her, she heaved, tidal, moon-driven." Eventually Miss Lonelyhearts "crawled out of bed like an exhausted swimmer leaving the surf," and she soon drags him back.

If Fay is an oceanic monster, Peter Doyle is only a sinister puppy. In bringing Miss Lonelyhearts back to the apartment at Fay's order, he half-jokes, "Ain't I the pimp, to bring home a guy for my wife?" Fay reacts by hitting him in the mouth with a rolled-up newspaper, and his comic response is to growl like a dog and catch the paper with his teeth. When she lets go of her end, he drops to his hands and knees and continues to imitate a dog on the floor. As Miss Lonelyhearts leans over to help him up, "Doyle tore open Miss Lonelyhearts' fly, then rolled over on his back, laughing wildly." Fay, more properly, accepts him as a dog and kicks him.

The obsessive theme of *Miss Lonelyhearts* is human pain and suffering, but it is represented almost entirely as female suffering. This is first spelled out in the letters addressed to Miss Lonelyhearts: Sick-of-it-all is a Roman Catholic wife who has had seven children in twelve years, is pregnant again, and has kidney pains so excruciating that she cries all the time. Desperate is a sixteen-year-old born with a hole in her face instead of a nose, who wants to have dates like other girls. Harold S. writes about his thirteen-year-old deaf-and-dumb sister Gracie, who was raped by a man when she was playing on the roof, and who will be brutally punished if her parents find out about it. Broad Shoulders was hit by a car when she was first pregnant, and is alternately persecuted and deserted by an unbalanced husband, in five pages of ghastly detail. Miss Lonelyhearts gets only two letters about male suffering, one from a paralyzed boy who wants to play the violin, the other from Peter Doyle, who complains of the pain from his crippled leg and the general meaninglessness of life.

The theme of indignities committed on women comes up in another form in the stories Miss Lonelyhearts' friends tell in Delehanty's. They seem to be exclusively anecdotes of group rape, of one woman gang-raped by eight neighbors, of another kept in the back room of a speakeasy for three days, until "on the last day they sold tickets to niggers." Miss Lonelyhearts identifies himself with "wife-torturers, rapers of small children." At one point he tries giving his readers the traditional Christian justification for suffering, that it is Christ's gift to mankind to bring them to Him, but he tears up the column.

Ultimately the novel cannot justify or even explain suffering, only proclaim its omnipresence. Lying sick in bed, Miss Lonelyhearts gets a vision of human life: "He found himself in the window of a pawnshop full of fur coats, diamond rings, watches, shotguns, fishing tackle, mandolins. All these things were the paraphernalia of suffering. A tortured high light twisted on the blade of a gift knife, a battered horn grunted with pain." Finally his mind forms everything into a gigantic cross, and he falls asleep exhausted.

The book's desperate cry of pain and suffering comes to a focus in what Miss Lonelyhearts calls his "Christ complex." He recognizes that Christ is the only answer to his readers' letters, but that "if he did not want to get sick, he had to stay away from the Christ business. Besides, Christ was Shrike's particular joke." As Miss Lonelyhearts leaves the office and walks through a little park, the shadow of a lamppost pierces his side like a spear. Since nothing grows in the park's battered earth, he decides to ask his correspondents to come and water the soil with their tears. He imagines Shrike telling him to teach them to pray each morning,

"Give us this day our daily stone," and thinks: "He had given his reader many stones; so many, in fact, that he had only one left — the stone that had formed in his gut."

Jesus Christ, Shrike says, is "the Miss Lonelyhearts of Miss Lonelyhearts." Miss Lonelyhearts has nailed an ivory Christ to the wall of his room with great spikes, but it disappoints him: "Instead of writhing, the Christ remained calmly decorative." Miss Lonelyhearts recalls: "As a boy in his father's church, he had discovered that something stirred in him when he shouted the name of Christ, something secret and enormously powerful." Unfortunately, he recognizes, it is not faith but hysteria: "For him, Christ was the most natural of excitements."

Miss Lonelyhearts tells Betty he is "a humanity lover," but Shrike more aptly identifies him a "leper licker." "If he could only believe in Christ," Miss Lonelyhearts thinks, "then everything would be simple and the letters extremely easy to answer." Later he recognizes that "Shrike had accelerated his sickness by teaching him to handle his one escape, Christ, with a thick glove of words." He decides that he has had a part in the general betrayal of suffering mankind: "The thing that made his share in it particularly bad was that he was capable of dreaming the Christ dream. He felt that he had failed at it, not so much because of Shrike's jokes or his own self-doubt, but because of his lack of humility." Miss Lonelyhearts concludes that "with him, even the word Christ was a vanity." When he gets drunk with Doyle, he calls on Christ joyously, and goes home with Doyle to bring the glad tidings to both Doyles, to heal their marriage. He preaches "love" to them and realizes that he is only writing another column, switches to preaching Christ Jesus, "the black fruit that hangs on the crosstree . . . the bidden fruit," and realizes that he is only echoing Shrike's poisoned rhetoric.

What Miss Lonelyhearts eventually achieves, since he cannot

believe in the real Christ, and refuses to become a spurious Christ, is Peter's condition. He becomes the rock on which the new church will be founded, but it is the church of catatonic withdrawal. After three days in bed Miss Lonelyhearts attains a state of perfect calm, and the stone in his gut expands until he becomes "an ancient rock, smooth with experience." The Shrikes come to take him to a party at their apartment, and against this rock the waves of Shrike dash in vain. When Mary wriggles on Miss Lonelyhearts' lap in the cab, "the rock remained perfect." At the party he withstands Shrike's newest mockery, the Miss Lonelyhearts Game, with indifference: "What goes on in the sea is of no interest to the rock." Miss Lonelyhearts leaves the party with Betty: "She too should see the rock he had become." He shamelessly promises her marriage and domesticity: "The rock was a solidification of his feeling, his conscience, his sense of reality, his self-knowledge." He then goes back to his sickbed content: "The rock had been thoroughly tested and had been found perfect."

The next day Miss Lonelyhearts is burning with fever, and "the rock became a furnace." The room fills with grace, the illusory grace of madness, and as Doyle comes up the stairs with a pistol Miss Lonelyhearts rushes downstairs to embrace him and heal his crippled leg, a miracle that will embody his succoring all suffering mankind with love. Unable to escape Miss Lonelyhearts' mad embrace, terrified by Betty coming up the stairs, Doyle tries to toss away the gun, and Miss Lonelyhearts is accidentally shot. He falls dragging Doyle down the stairs in his arms.

It is of course a homosexual tableau — the men locked in embrace while the woman stands helplessly by — and behind his other miseries Miss Lonelyhearts has a powerful latent homosexuality. It is this that is ultimately the joke of his name and the book's title. It explains his acceptance of teasing dates with Mary and his coldness with Mary; he thinks of her excitement and notes: "No similar change ever took place in his own body, however. Like a dead man, only friction could make him warm or violence make him mobile." It explains his discontent with Betty. Most of all it explains his joy at being seduced by Fay — "He had always been the pursuer, but now found a strange pleasure in have the roles reversed" — and how quickly the pleasure turns to disgust.

The communion Miss Lonelyhearts achieves with Doyle in Delehanty's consists in their sitting silently holding hands, Miss Lonelyhearts pressing "with all the love he could manage" to overcome the revulsion he feels at Doyle's touch. Back at the Doyles, after Doyle has ripped open Miss Lonelyhearts' fly and been kicked by his wife, they hold hands again, and when Fay comes back in the room she says "What a sweet pair of fairies you guys are." It is West's ultimate irony that the symbolic embrace they manage at the end is one penetrating the body of the other with a bullet.

We could, if we so chose, write Miss Lonelyhearts' case history before the novel begins. Terrified of his stern religious father, identifying with his soft loving mother, the boy renounces his phallicism out of castration anxiety — a classic Oedipus complex. In these terms the Shrikes are Miss Lonelyhearts' Oedipal parents, abstracted as the father's loud voice and the mother's tantalizing breast. The scene at the end of Miss Lonelyhearts' date with Mary Shrike is horrifying and superb. Standing outside her apartment door, suddenly overcome with passion, he strips her naked under her fur coat while she keeps talking mindlessly of her mother's death, mumbling and repeating herself, so that Shrike will not hear their sudden silence and come out. Finally Mary agrees to let Miss Lonelyhearts in if Shrike is not home, goes inside, and soon Shrike peers out the door, wearing only the top of his pajamas. It is the child's Oedipal vision perfectly dramatized: he

23

can clutch at his mother's body but loses her each time to his more potent rival.

It should be noted that if this is the pattern of Miss Lonelyhearts' Oedipus complex, it is not that of West, nor are the Shrikes the pattern of West's parents. How conscious was West of all or any of this? I would guess, from the book's title, that he was entirely conscious of at least Miss Lonelyhearts' latent homosexuality. As for the Oedipus complex, all one can do is note West's remarks in "Some Notes on Miss Lonelyhearts": "Psychology has nothing to do with reality nor should it be used as motivation. The novelist is no longer a psychologist. Psychology can become much more important. The great body of case histories can be used in the way the ancient writers use their myths. Freud is your Bulfinch; you can not learn from him."

The techniques West uses to express his themes are perfectly suited to them. The most important is a pervasive desperate and savage tone, not only in the imagery of violence and suffering, but everywhere. It is the tone of a world where unreason is triumphant. Telling Miss Lonelyhearts that he is awaiting a girl "of great intelligence," Shrike "illustrated the word *intelligence* by carving two enormous breasts in the air with his hands." When Miss Lonelyhearts is in the country with Betty, a gas station attendant tells him amiably that "it wasn't the hunters who drove out the deer, but the yids." When Miss Lonelyhearts accidentally collides with a man in Delehanty's and turns to apologize, he is punched in the mouth.

The flowering cactus that blooms in this wasteland is Shrike's rhetoric. The book begins with a mock prayer he has composed for Miss Lonelyhearts, and every time Shrike appears he makes a masterly speech: on religion, on escapes, on the gospel of Miss Lonelyhearts according to Shrike. He composes a mock letter to God, in which Miss Lonelyhearts confesses shyly: "I read your column and like it very much." He is a cruel and relentless punster and wit. In his sadistic game at the party, Shrike reads aloud letters to Miss Lonelyhearts. He reads one from a pathetic old woman who sells pencils for a living, and concludes: "She has rheum in her eyes. Have you room in your heart for her?" He reads another, from the paralyzed boy who wants to play the violin, and concludes: "How pathetic! However, one can learn much from this parable. Label the boy Labor, the violin Capital, and so on . . ." Shrike's masterpiece, the brilliant evocation of the ultimate inadequacy of such escapes as the soil, the South Seas, Hedonism, and art, is a classic of modern rhetoric, as is his shorter speech on religion. Here are a few sentences from the latter: "Under the skin of man is a wondrous jungle where veins like lush tropical growths hang along overripe organs and weed-like entrails writhe in squirming tangles of red and yellow. In this jungle, flitting from rock-gray lungs to golden intestines, from liver to lights and back to liver again, lives a bird called the soul. The Catholic hunts this bird with bread and wine, the Hebrew with a golden ruler, the Protestant on leaden feet with leaden words, the Buddhist with gestures, the Negro with blood."

The other cactus that flowers in the wasteland is sadistic violence. The book's most harrowing chapter, "Miss Lonelyhearts and the lamb," is a dream or recollection of a college escapade, in which Miss Lonelyhearts and two other boys, after drinking all night, buy a lamb to barbecue in the woods. Miss Lonelyhearts persuades his companions to sacrifice it to God before barbecuing it. They lay the lamb on a flower-covered altar and Miss Lonelyhearts tries to cut its throat, but succeeds only in maiming it and breaking the knife. The lamb escapes and crawls off into the underbrush, and the boys flee. Later Miss Lonelyhearts goes back and crushes the lamb's head with a stone. This nightmarish scene, with its unholy suggestions of the sacrifices of Isaac and Christ, embodies the book's bitter paradox: that sadism is the perversion of love.

Visiting Betty early in the novel, aware "that only violence could make him supple," Miss Lonelyhearts reaches inside her robe and tugs at her nipple unpleasantly. "Let me pluck this rose," he says, "I want to wear it in my buttonhole." In "Miss Lonelyhearts and the clean old man," he and a drunken friend find an old gentleman in a washroom, drag him to a speakeasy, and torment him with questions about his "homosexualistic tendencies." As they get nastier and nastier, Miss Lonelyhearts feels "as he had felt years before, when he had accidentally stepped on a small frog. Its spilled guts had filled him with pity, but when its suffering had become real to his senses, his pity had turned to rage and he had beaten it frantically until it was dead." He ends by twisting the old man's arm until the old man screams and someone hits Miss Lonelyhearts with a chair.

The book's only interval of decency, beauty, and peace is the pastoral idyll of the few days Miss Lonelyhearts spends with Betty in the country. They drive in a borrowed car to the deserted farmhouse in Connecticut where she was born. It is spring, and Miss Lonelyhearts "had to admit, even to himself, that the pale new leaves, shaped and colored like candle flames, were beautiful and that the air smelt clean and alive." They work at cleaning up the place, Betty cooks simple meals, and they go down to the pond to watch the deer. After they eat an apple that has ominous Biblical overtones, Betty reveals that she is a virgin and they go fraternally to bed. The next day they go for a naked swim; then, with "no wind to disturb the pull of the earth," Betty is ceremonially deflowered on the new grass. The reader is repeatedly warned that natural innocence cannot save Miss Lonelyhearts: the noise of birds and crickets is "a horrible racket" in his ears; in the woods, "in the deep shade there was nothing but death —

rotten leaves, gray and white fungi, and over everything a funereal hush." When they get back to New York, "Miss Lonelyhearts knew that Betty had failed to cure him and that he had been right when he had said that he could never forget the letters." Later, when Miss Lonelyhearts is a rock and leaves Shrike's party with Betty, he tries to create a miniature idyll of innocence by taking her out for a strawberry soda, but it fails. Pregnant by him and intending to have an abortion, Betty remains nevertheless in Edenic innocence; Miss Lonelyhearts is irretrievably fallen, and there is no savior who can redeem.

The book's pace is frantic and its imagery is garish, ugly, and compelling. The letters to Miss Lonelyhearts are "stamped from the dough of suffering with a heart-shaped cookie knife." The sky looks "as if it had been rubbed with a soiled eraser." A bloodshot eye in the peephole of Delehanty's glows "like a ruby in an antique iron ring." Finishing his sermon to the "intelligent" girl, Shrike "buried his triangular face like the blade of a hatchet in her neck." Miss Lonelyhearts' tongue is "a fat thumb," his heart "a congealed lump of icy fat," and his only feeling "icy fatness." Goldsmith, a colleague at the paper, has cheeks "like twin rolls of smooth pink toilet paper." Only the imagery of the Connecticut interlude temporarily thaws the iciness and erases the unpleasant associations with fatness and thumb. As Miss Lonelyhearts watches Betty naked, "She looked a little fat, but when she lifted something to the line, all the fat disappeared. Her raised arms pulled her breasts up until they were like pink-tipped thumbs."

The unique greatness of *Miss Lonelyhearts* seems to have come into the world with hardly a predecessor, but it has itself influenced a great many American novelists since. *Miss Lonelyhearts* seems to me one of the three finest American novels of our century. The other two are F. Scott Fitzgerald's *The Great Gatsby* and Ernest Hemingway's *The Sun Also Rises.* It shares with them a lost and victimized hero, a bitter sense of our civilization's falsity, a pervasive melancholy atmosphere of failure and defeat. If the tone of *Miss Lonelyhearts* is more strident, its images more garish, its pace more rapid and hysterical, it is as fitting an epitome of the thirties as they are of the twenties. If nothing in the forties and fifties has similarly gone beyond *Miss Lonelyhearts* in violence and shock, it may be because it stands at the end of the line.

A Cool Million, subtitled "The Dismantling of Lemuel Pitkin," is a comic, even a parody, novel, to some extent a reversion to the world of *Balso Snell.* It tells the story of Lemuel Pitkin, a poor but honest Vermont boy, as he attempts to make his way in the world. As he confronts each experience with the old-fashioned virtues of honesty, sobriety, good sportsmanship, thrift, bravery, chivalry, and kindness, he is robbed, beaten up, mutilated, cheated, and victimized. In an interwoven subplot, Elizabeth Prail, a neighbor who similarly represents decent American girlhood, is sexually mistreated: raped, beaten by a sadist, kidnapped by white slavers and sold into prostitution, turned out to walk the streets, and so forth. Meanwhile their town banker, "Shagpoke" Whipple, a former President of the United States, creates an American fascist movement and takes over the country.

The total effect is that of a prolonged, perhaps overprolonged, jape. The stages of the action are the stages of Lem's dismantling: thrown into jail in a frame-up, he loses all his teeth because the warden believes teeth to be the source of moral infection; rescuing a banker and his daughter from a runaway horse, Lem loses an eye; kidnapped by agents of the Communist International, he is involved in an automobile collision and loses a thumb; trying to save Betty from rape, he is caught in a bear trap that the villain has planted, which costs him a leg, and while unconscious in the trap he is scalped by a Harvard-educated Indian. He is eventually hired as stooge for a vaudeville act and demolished during each performance; when he is hit with a mallet, "His toupee flew off, his eye and teeth popped out, and his wooden leg was knocked into the audience." Eventually Lem is shot down onstage while making a speech for American fascism. As a result of his martyrdom Whipple's Leather Shirts triumph, and Pitkin's Birthday becomes a national holiday, on which the youth of America parade singing "The Lemuel Pitkin Song."

What form the book has comes from these ritual stages of dismemberment, but in a truer sense *A Cool Million* is formless, an inorganic stringing together of comic set-pieces, with the preposterous incidents serving merely to raise the various topics West chooses to satirize. Thus Betty's residence in Wu Fong's brothel sets off pages of comic description, first of the brothel as a House of All Nations, then, when Wu Fong is converted by the "Buy American" campaign of the Hearst newspapers, into an all-American establishment. West joyously describes the regional costumes and decor of each girl at considerable length, concluding with the cuisine: "When a client visited Lena Haubengrauber, it was possible for him to eat roast groundhog and drink Sam Thompson rye. While with Alice Sweethorne, he was served sow belly with grits and bourbon. In Mary Judkins' room he received, if he so desired, fried squirrel and corn liquor. In the suite occupied by Patricia Van Riis, lobster and champagne wine were the rule. The patrons of Powder River Rose usually ordered mountain oysters and washed them down with forty-rod. And so on down the list: while with Dolores O'Riely, tortillas and prune brandy from the Imperial Valley; while with Princess Roan Fawn, baked dog and firewater; while with Betty Prail, fish chowder and Jamaica rum. Finally, those who sought the favors of the 'Modern

Girl,' Miss Cobina Wiggs, were regaled with tomato and lettuce sandwiches and gin."

The introduction of a Pike County "ring-tail squealer" and "rip-tail roarer" gives West an opportunity to improvise tall talk and anecdotes concluding: "His bones are bleachin' in the canyon where he fell." The Indian chief who scalps Lem is a Spenglerian philosopher and critic of our gadget civilization, and his speech to the tribe to rouse them for the warpath is a long comic diatribe, culminating in: "But now all the secret places of the earth are full. Now even the Grand Canyon will no longer hold razor blades." Later Lem and Whipple join up with a traveling show exhibiting a Chamber of American Horrors, and West gives himself a chance to describe some of the horrors of American life In one exhibit, all the materials are disguised: "Paper had been made to look like wood, wood like rubber, rubber like steel, steel like cheese, cheese like glass, and, finally, glass like paper." In another, function is disguised: "The visitor saw flower pots that were really victrolas, revolvers that held candy, candy that held collar buttons and so forth." West here is entirely indiscriminate. The accompanying pageant of American history consists of sketches "in which Quakers were shown being branded, Indians brutalized and cheated, Negroes sold, children sweated to death," as though these acts were on the order of disguising paper to look like wood.

It is at once comic and depressing, the fitting work of a man Robert M. Coates has called "the most thoroughly pessimistic person I have ever known." If its indictment of American material civilization does not go very deep, its awareness of the precariousness of American freedom does, and the book is perhaps strongest as a political warning. Writing just after the accession of Hitler, West felt the vulnerability of America to totalitarianism disguised as superpatriotism, and he makes it disturbingly convincing. Whipple's bands of the mindless and disaffected, got up in fringed deerskin shirts, coonskin caps, and squirrel rifles, are the same joke as Lena Haubengrauber's clients washing down roast groundhog with Sam Thompson rye, but here it images our nightmare. Recruiting on street corners, Whipple alternates appeals to destroy the Jewish international bankers and the Bolshevik labor unions with shouts of "Remember the Alamo! Remember the Maine!" and "Back to the principles of Andy Jackson and Abe Lincoln!"

In his final tribute to the martyred Lemuel Pitkin at the end of the book, as his storm troops parade down Fifth Avenue, Whipple makes it clear that the true enemy from which his National Revolutionary party has delivered the country is "sophistication." Lem's life represented the expectations of American innocence, frustrated by "sophisticated aliens," and the revolution has been made by those who share Lem's expectations. As such it is the revolt of the frustrated and tormented lower middle class, a fantasy foreshadowing of the riot at the end of *The Day of the Locust*. To become the Horst Wessel of American fascism, in West's ugliest joke, Lem has stepped out of a Norman Rockwell cover for the *Saturday Evening Post*.

What makes this cautionary tale convincing in *A Cool Million* is West's sense of the pervasiveness of American violence. It is like the savagery of Russian life in Leskov or Gorki. We see Betty Prail at twelve, the night her family's house burns down and her parents are killed in the fire. When the firemen finally arrive, drunk, they do nothing to put out the fire. Instead they loot the house while the chief rapes Betty, leaving her naked and unconscious on the ground. She is then sent to an orphan asylum, and put out at fourteen to be a maid in the household of Deacon Slemp, where in addition to her other duties she is enthusiastical-

31

ly beaten twice a week on the bare behind by the Deacon, who gives her a quarter after each beating.

In this world where firemen are looters and rapists and church elders perverts and hypocrites, policemen appear only to beat up the victims of crimes. When Lem is first seized by the police, on his way to the big city to make his fortune, a patrolman clubs him on the head, one detective kicks him in the stomach, and a second kicks him behind the ear; all three actions unrelated to any of the remarks they make to Lem, but rather, natural reflexes. When Lem faints from the wound he received from stopping the runaway horse, he is found by a policeman, who establishes communication by kicking him in the groin. The brutal image of the police in the book is always the raised truncheon, the doubled fist, the foot drawn back.

The weaknesses of the book are perhaps the inevitable weaknesses of the form, jokes that do not come off and failures of tone. Sometimes the book is almost unbelievably corny and heavy-handed. When he is in this mood, West will even have someone address a Chinese in pidgin and be answered in flawless English.

The uncertainty of tone is mainly in regard to sex. When West is openly vulgar, he is fine, but on occasion he seems to smirk, and then he is less fine. A scene between Lem, captured by Wu Fong's men, dressed in a tight-fitting sailor suit, and set up as a homosexual prostitute in the brothel, and his client, a lisping Indian maharajah, is perhaps the most extreme failure. The first rape of Betty by the drunken fire chief is disturbing and effective, but her thousandth rape is boring and meaningless, as comedy, social comment, or even titillation. Betty is almost invariably unconscious when raped, an oddly necrophiliac touch, and sometimes the details lead us to expect a salacious illustration on the next page.

West's last book, *The Day of the Locust* (1939), is a novel about a young painter named Tod Hackett, working at a Hollywood movie studio as a set and costume designer, and some people he encounters. These are principally Faye Greener, a beautiful young girl whom he loves; her father Harry, an old vaudeville comic; Earle Shoop, Faye's cowboy beau; Miguel, Earle's Mexican friend who breeds fighting cocks; Abe Kusich, a dwarf racetrack tout; and Homer Simpson, an innocent from the Midwest also in love with Faye. In the course of the novel Harry dies, and Faye and her friends go to live with Homer. The action is climaxed by a wild party at Homer's, after which Faye and Miguel end up in bed. This results, the next day, in Homer's demented murder of a boy, which in turn precipitates a riot in the streets, on which the book ends. The title comes from the plague of locusts visited on Pharaoh in the Book of Exodus.

Like the characters in *Miss Lonelyhearts*, the characters in *The Day of the Locust* tend to be symbolic abstractions, but here with some loss of human reality. Tod, who never quite comes to life (mainly, I think, because of West's efforts to keep him from being autobiographical), represents The Painter's Eye. All through the book he is planning a great canvas, "The Burning of Los Angeles," which will sum up the whole violent and demented civilization. It is to show the city burning at high noon, set on fire by a gay holiday crowd, who appear carrying baseball bats and torches: "No longer bored, they sang and danced joyously in the red light of the flames." In the foreground, Tod and his friends flee the mob in various characteristic postures: Faye naked and running rather proudly, throwing her knees high; Homer half-asleep; Tod stopping to throw a stone at the crowd. Meanwhile the flames lick avidly "at a corinthian column that held up the palmleaf roof of a nutburger stand."

Faye is nothing like the Fay of *Miss Lonelyhearts* (as the Betty of *A Cool Million* is nothing like the Betty of *Miss Lonelyhearts*

— West was overeconomical of names). Faye is seventeen, "a tall girl with wide, straight shoulders and long, swordlike legs." She has "a moon face, wide at the cheek bones and narrow at chin and brow," her hair is platinum-blonde, her breasts are "placed wide apart and their thrust" is "upward and outward," her buttocks look "like a heart upside down." She dresses like a child of twelve, eats an apple with her little finger curled, and has a brain the size of a walnut.

Like Betty in *Miss Lonelyhearts,* Faye represents Nature, but now Nature's appearance of innocence is seen as deceptive, and Faye is as far as can be from Betty. Tod looks at an inviting photograph of her, lying "with her arms and legs spread, as though welcoming a lover," and thinks: "Her invitation wasn't to pleasure, but to struggle, hard and sharp, closer to murder than to love. If you threw yourself on her, it would be like throwing yourself from the parapet of a skyscraper. You would do it with a scream. You couldn't expect to rise again. Your teeth would be driven into your skull like nails into a pine board and your back would be broken. You wouldn't even have time to sweat or close your eyes." What then is Tod's conclusion? "If she would only let him, he would be glad to throw himself, no matter what the cost." Luckily, she never lets him.

All experience rolls off Faye. She smells to Tod like "buckwheat in flower"; when she leans toward him, drooping slightly, "he had seen young birches droop like that at midday when they are over-heavy with sun." When she announces her intention of becoming a call girl, Tod decides that "her beauty was structural like a tree's, not a quality of her mind or heart. Perhaps even whoring wouldn't damage it for that reason." A spell of whoring does not in fact damage it, and when Tod sees her later: "She looked just born, everything moist and fresh, volatile and perfumed." In her natural acceptance of the world of sexuality, she *is*, as Homer tells Tod proudly, "a fine, wholesome child."

This vision of Nature emphasizes its infuriating invulnerability, and Tod not only wants to smash himself on it, but in other moods, to smash Faye. He thinks: "If he only had the courage to throw himself on her. Nothing less violent than rape would do. The sensation he felt was like that he got when holding an egg in his hand. Not that she was fragile or even seemed fragile. It wasn't that. It was her completeness, her egglike self-sufficiency, that made him want to crush her." Seeing her again, Tod feels: "Her self-sufficiency made him squirm and the desire to break its smooth surface with a blow, or at least a sudden obscene gesture, became irresistible." When Faye disappears at the end of the book, Tod cannot decide whether she has gone off with Miguel or gone back to being a call girl. "But either way she would come out all right," he thinks. "Nothing could hurt her. She was like a cork. No matter how rough the sea got, she would go dancing over the same waves that sank iron ships and tore away piers of reinforced concrete." Tod then produces an elaborate fantasy of waiting in a parking lot to knock Faye unconscious and rape her, and he steps from that into the riot of the book's last scene.

The men around Faye are in their different fashions as mindless as she. Her father, Harry Greener, after forty years in vaudeville and burlesque, no longer has any personality apart from his clowning role. "It was his sole method of defense," West explains. "Most people, he had discovered, won't go out of their way to punish a clown." West invents a superb clown act for him, presented in the form of an old clipping from the Sunday *Times,* but the clowning we see in the book is of a more poignant sort, his comic act peddling home-made silver polish.

Faye's cowboy, Earle Shoop, is an image of virile idiocy. "He had a two-dimensional face that a talented child might have drawn with a ruler and a compass. His chin was perfectly round and his eyes, which were wide apart, were also round. His thin mouth ran at right angles to his straight, perpendicular nose. His reddish tan complexion was the same color from hairline to throat, as though washed in by an expert, and it completed his resemblance to a mechanical drawing." His conversation consists of "Lo, thar," "Nope," and "I was only funning."

The Mexican, Miguel, is an image of pure sensuality: "He was toffee-colored with large Armenian eyes and pouting black lips. His head was a mass of tight, ordered curls." When Faye responds to him, "his skin glowed and the oil in his black curls sparkled." Early in the book we see him rhumba with Faye, until jealousy drives Earle to smash him over the head with a stick. Later he tangos with her, a tango that ends in bed. "Mexicans are very good with women," Tod decides, as the moral of the episode.

Homer is the most completely abstracted character in the book. As Mary Shrike in *Miss Lonelyhearts* is entirely reduced to Breasts, so Homer is entirely reduced to an image of Hands, enormous hands independent of his body. We see him waking in the morning: "Every part was awake but his hands. They still slept. He was not surprised. They demanded special attention, had always demanded it. When he had been a child, he used to stick pins into them and once had even thrust them into a fire. Now he used only cold water." We see him plunge his hands into the washbasin: "They lay quietly on the bottom like a pair of strange aquatic animals. When they were thoroughly chilled and began to crawl about, he lifted them out and hid them in a towel." In the bath: "He kept his enormous hands folded quietly on his belly. Although absolutely still, they seemed curbed rather than resting." When Homer cuts his hand opening a can, "The wounded hand writhed about on the kitchen table until it was carried to the sink by its mate and bathed tenderly in hot water."

When Faye cries at their first meeting, Homer makes "his big hands dance at the end of his arms," and "several times his hands moved forward to comfort her, but he succeeded in curbing them." As he and Faye sit and eat: "His hands began to bother him. He rubbed them against the edge of the table to relieve their itch, but it only stimulated them. When he clasped them behind his back, the strain became intolerable. They were hot and swollen. Using the dishes as an excuse, he held them under the cold water tap of the sink." When Faye leaves, Homer is too bashful to say anything affectionate, but: "His hands were braver. When Faye shook good-bye, they clutched and refused to let go." After she leaves, "His hands kept his thoughts busy. They trembled and jerked, as though troubled by dreams. To hold them still, he clasped them together. Their fingers twined like a tangle of thighs in miniature. He snatched them apart and sat on them."

This garish and remarkable image is built up throughout the book to embody all of Homer's repressed violence; the hands are strangler's hands, rapist's hands. For reasons impossible to imagine or justify, West let it all go to waste. When Homer's violence finally does break out, when Faye's leaving has driven him out of his mind, he kills a boy who has hit him in the face with a stone by stomping him to death, never touching him with his hands.

The most grotesque character in this gallery of grotesques is the dwarf, Abe Kusich. When Tod first meets him, he is wearing perfect dwarf headgear, a high green Tyrolean hat. Unfortunately, "the rest of his outfit didn't go well with the hat. Instead of shoes with long points and a leather apron, he wore a blue, double-breasted suit and a black shirt with a yellow tie. Instead of a crooked thorn stick, he carried a rolled copy of the *Daily Running Horse*." His tiny size is made pathetic in an image of his catching Tod's attention by tugging at the bottom of his jacket, but it is accompanied by an unbelievable pugnacity, verbal and physical. He is a small murderous animal like Homer's hands, and he too finally erupts into violence, responding to a kick in the stomach from Earle by squeezing Earle's testicles until he collapses.

West's earlier title for *The Day of the Locust* was *The Cheated*, and the latent violence of the cheated, the mob that fires Los Angeles in Tod's picture, and riots in the flesh at the end of the book, is its major theme. The cheated are recognizable by sight in Hollywood: "Their clothing was somber and badly cut, bought from mail-order houses." They stand on the streets staring at passers-by, and "when their stare was returned, their eyes filled with hatred." They are the people who have "come to California to die." At one point Tod wonders "if he weren't exaggerating the importance of the people who come to California to die. Maybe they weren't really desperate enough to set a single city on fire, let alone the whole country." His ultimate discovery is that they are.

Some of the cheated come to Harry's funeral, "hoping for a dramatic incident of some sort, hoping at least for one of the mourners to be led weeping hysterically from the chapel." As he stares at them, "it seemed to Tod that they stared back at him with an expression of vicious, acrid boredom that trembled on the edge of violence." In the book's last scene, the cheated line up by the thousands outside Kahn's Persian Palace Theatre for the première of a new picture. The mob terrifies Tod, and he now recognizes it as a demonic collective entity, unstoppable once aroused except by machine guns. In one of West's rare Marxist slantings, the mob includes no workingmen, but is entirely "made up of the lower middle classes." Tod concludes:

"It was a mistake to think them harmless curiosity seekers.

They were savage and bitter, especially the middle-aged and the old, and had been made so by boredom and disappointment.

"All their lives they had slaved at some kind of dull, heavy labor, behind desks and counters, in the fields and at tedious machines of all sorts, saving their pennies and dreaming of the leisure that would be theirs when they had enough. Finally that day came. They could draw a weekly income of ten or fifteen dollars. Where else should they go but California, the land of sunshine and oranges?

"Once there, they discovered that sunshine isn't enough. They get tired of oranges, even of avocado pears and passion fruit. Nothing happens. They don't know what to do with their time. They haven't the mental equipment for leisure, the money nor the physical equipment for pleasure. Did they slave so long just to go on an occasional Iowa picnic? What else is there? They watch the waves come in at Venice. There wasn't any ocean where most of them came from, but after you've seen one wave you've seen them all. The same is true of the airplanes at Glendale. If only a plane would crash once in a while so that they could watch the passengers being consumed in a 'holocaust of flame,' as the newspapers put it. But the planes never crash.

"Their boredom becomes more and more terrible. They realize that they've been tricked and burn with resentment. Every day of their lives they read the newspapers and went to the movies. Both fed them on lynchings, murder, sex crimes, explosions, wrecks, love nests, fires, miracles, revolutions, wars. This daily diet made sophisticates of them. The sun is a joke. Oranges can't titillate their jaded palates. Nothing can ever be violent enough to make taut their slack minds and bodies. They have been cheated and betrayed. They have slaved and saved for nothing."

As the marching Leather Shirts were West's fantasy of American fascism, this vicious mob of the cheated lower middle class is

39

his fantasy of American democracy, and it is overpowering and terrifying. The rest of Hollywood, the cheaters, have no more cultural identity than the "cheated," but their plight is comic or pathetic rather than menacing. They inhabit the Chamber of American Horrors, come to life. They live in "Mexican ranch houses, Samoan huts, Mediterranean villas, Egyptian and Japanese temples, Swiss chalets, Tudor cottages, and every possible combination of these styles." Tod sees "a miniature Rhine castle with tarpaper turrets pierced for archers. Next to it was a little highly colored shack with domes and minarets out of the *Arabian Nights*." The house Homer rents is Irish peasant style: "It had an enormous and very crooked stone chimney, little dormer windows with big hoods and a thatched roof that came down very low on both sides of the front door. This door was of gumwood painted like fumed oak and it hung on enormous hinges. Although made by machine, the hinges had been carefully stamped to appear hand-forged. The same kind of care and skill had been used to make the roof thatching, which was not really straw but heavy fireproof paper colored and ribbed to look like straw." The living room is "Spanish," with red and gold silk armorial banners and a plaster galleon; the bedrooms "New England," with spool beds made of iron grained like wood.

The people are as spurious as the houses and things. An old Hollywood Indian called Chief Kiss-My-Towkus speaks a language of "Vas you dere, Sharley?" Human communication is impossible anywhere in Hollywood. At a party of movie people, the men go off to talk shop and at least one woman assumes that they are telling dirty jokes. Harry and Faye are unable to quarrel in words, but have bitter wordless battles in which he laughs insanely, she sings and dances. Even Faye's sensual gesture of wetting her lips with her tongue as she smiles is meaningless. At first Tod takes it to be an invitation, and dreams: "Her lips must taste of blood and salt." Eventually he discovers the truth: "It was one of her most characteristic gestures and very effective. It seemed to promise all sorts of undefined intimacies, yet it was really as simple and automatic as the word thanks. She used it to reward anyone for anything, no matter how unimportant."

One of the clues West gives to his conception of the nature and destiny of his characters is subtly dropped in a comic scene. Tod and Homer meet a neighbor of Homer's, Maybelle Loomis, and her eight-year-old son, Adore, whom she has trained as a performer. He is dressed as an adult, his eyebrows are plucked, and he sings a salacious song with a mechanical counterfeit of sexuality: "When he came to the final chorus, his buttocks writhed and his voice carried a top-heavy load of sexual pain." In a more personal display, Adore makes horrible faces at Homer, and Mrs. Loomis apologizes: "He thinks he's the Frankenstein monster." Adore *is* the Frankenstein monster, and it is he who is killed by Homer in the book's last scene. But Homer too is the Frankenstein monster, getting out of bed "in sections, like a poorly made automaton," and his hands are progeny monsters. Earle is a lesser monster, a wound-up cowboy toy, and Miguel is a phallic Jack-in-the-box. More than any of them, Faye is a Frankenstein monster, a mechanical woman self-created from bits of vanished film heroines, and her invulnerability is the invulnerability of the already dead. Here is the novel's deepest indictment of the American civilization it symbolizes in Hollywood: if the rubes are cheated by the image of an artificially colored orange, Tod is more deeply cheated by a zombie love; our dreams are fantasies of death.

In his article "Some Notes on Violence," published in *Contact* in 1932, West writes: "What is melodramatic in European writing is not necessarily so in American writing. For a European writer to make violence real, he has to do a great deal of careful psychology and sociology. He often needs three hundred pages to

41

motivate one little murder. But not so the American writer. His audience has been prepared and is neither surprised nor shocked if he omits artistic excuses for familiar events." The action of *The Day of the Locust* is the releasing of springs of violence that have been wound too tight: Abe's sexual maiming of Earle, Miguel smashing Abe against the wall in retaliation, Homer's brutal murder of Adore, the riot of the cheated. All of these are directly or indirectly inspired by Faye: Earle and Abe and Miguel are competing for Faye, Faye has made Homer insane, Homer's act triggers the mob's insanity.

The party scene consists of a progressive stripping of Faye. She receives her five male guests wearing a pair of green silk lounging pajamas with the top three buttons open. By the time she dances with Miguel all the buttons are open. In the succeeding fight her pajamas are badly torn, and she takes off the trousers, revealing tight black lace drawers. When Homer finds her in bed with Miguel, she is naked. It beautifully represents a metaphoric stripping of Faye in the course of the book. Darwin writes that we observe the face of Nature "bright with gladness," and forget the war to the death behind its innocent appearance. Faye is that bright glad face of Nature, and the stripping gradually reveals the violence and death her beauty conceals. The novel is a great unmasking of a death's head.

West's literary techniques in *The Day of the Locust* develop organically out of his themes. The imagery for Hollywood is wild and surrealist. Tod's friend Claude Estee, a successful screen writer, has a lifesize rubber dead horse, bloated and putrefying, in his swimming pool. The supermarket plays colored spotlights on the food: "The oranges were bathed in red, the lemons in yellow, the fish in pale green, the steaks in rose and the eggs in ivory." As Tod walks through the movie lot looking for Faye, it becomes the nightmare of history: stepping through the swinging door of a Western saloon, he finds himself in a Paris street; crossing a bridge marked "To Kamp Komfit," he finds himself in a Greek temple; he walks on, "skirting the skeleton of a Zeppelin, a bamboo stockade, an adobe fort, the wooden horse of Troy, a flight of baroque palace stairs that started in a bed of weeds and ended against the branches of an oak, part of the Fourteenth Street elevated station, a Dutch windmill, the bones of a dinosaur, the upper half of the Merrimac, a corner of a Mayan temple." "A dream dump," he concludes. "A Sargasso of the imagination!"

"Having known something of the Hollywood West saw at the time he was seeing it," Allan Seager has written, "I am of the opinion that *Locust* was not fantasy imagined but fantasy seen." Although West probably invented the specific details of the dead horse and the pale green supermarket fish, the fireproof paper thatch and his old favorite the Trojan Horse, there is a sense in which Seager's remark is true: these things are no more garish than what West actually did see in Hollywood. West's technique in the book is often, as Seager suggests, what the artists call *objets trouvés*: he finds in reality the symbol he needs, rather than creating it. When *The Day of the Locust* appeared, I recall thinking how masterfully West had invented the bloody sex-drenched details of the cockfight that leads up to the book's final party. Having since been to cockfights, I now know that every symbolic detail was realistically observed, and the object of my admiration in connection with the scene is no longer West's brilliance of invention but his brilliance of selection.

The humor of the book arises out of its themes, the incongruities of Hollywood and its lack of a cultural identity. Standing on the porch of his plantation mansion, Claude Estee cries, "Here, you black rascal! A mint julep," and a Chinese servant promptly brings a Scotch and soda. What do the Gingos, an Eskimo family brought to Hollywood to make retakes of an Arctic film, eat? Naturally, smoked salmon, white fish, and marinated herring, bought at Jewish delicatessens. The spoken language in the book is a tribute to the delicacy of West's ear. It includes Harry Greener's vaudeville jargon: "Joe was laying up with a whisker in the old Fifth Avenue when the stove exploded. It was the broad's husband who blew the whistle." Along with it there is the very different belligerent idiom of Abe Kusich, shouting "No quiff can give Abe Kusich the fingeroo and get away with it," calling Earle a "pee-hole bandit," or boasting after he has incapacitated him, "I fixed that buckeroo." At the same time there is the witty and epigrammatic conversation of Claude and Tod. Typically, Claude describes Mrs. Jenning's brothel as "a triumph of industrial design," Tod answers that he nevertheless finds it depressing, "like all places for deposit, banks, mail boxes, tombs, vending machines," and Claude then improvises on that set theme. Claude is clearly West's ideal vision of himself: "He was master of an involved comic rhetoric that permitted him to express his moral indignation and still keep his reputation for worldliness and wit."

Some of the images in the book are as powerful as any in *Miss Lonelyhearts*. One is bird blood. We see it first as Earle plucks some quail: "Their feathers fell to the ground, point first, weighed down by the tiny drop of blood that trembled on the tips of their quills." It reappears magnified and horrible as the losing cock's beak breaks: "A large bubble of blood rose where the beak had been." Another powerful image is of Homer crying, at first making a sound "like that of a dog lapping gruel," then in his madness sobbing "like an ax chopping pine, a heavy, hollow, chunking noise." A third image is the scene of male communion between Tod and Homer, resembling that between Miss Lonelyhearts and Doyle, and like it a prelude to violence. Tod and Homer

44

leave the party to sit out on the curb, and Homer sits inarticulate, with a "sweet grin on his face," then takes Tod's hand and makes "trembling signals of affection."

The book's most vivid sustained image, perhaps more powerful than anything in *Miss Lonelyhearts,* is the riot, which is nightmarishly sexual as well as threatening. Swept along by the mob, Tod is thrown against a young girl whose clothes have been half torn off. With her thigh between his legs, she clings to him, and he discovers that she is being attacked from behind by an old man who has a hand inside her dress and is biting her neck. When Tod frees her from the old man, she is seized by another man, as Tod is swept impotently by. In another part of the crowd, they are talking with delight of a pervert who ripped up a girl with a pair of scissors, as they hug and pinch one another. Tod finally kicks off a woman trying to hang on to him, and escapes with no more than his leg broken, and a vision of the mob for his painting as "a great united front of screwballs and screwboxes."

Despite this and other very powerful scenes, I think that *The Day of the Locust* ultimately fails as a novel. Shifting from Tod to Homer and back to Tod, it has no dramatic unity, and in comparison with *Miss Lonelyhearts,* it has no moral core. Where Miss Lonelyhearts' inability to stay in Betty's Eden is heartbreaking, Tod's disillusion with Faye is only sobering, and where the end of the former is tragic, the end of this, Tod in the police car screaming along with the siren, is merely hysteric.

There is humor but little joy in West's novels, obsessive sexuality but few consummations (except for that sit-up-and-lie-down doll Betty Prail). The world West shows us is for the most part repulsive and terrifying. It is his genius to have found objective correlatives for our sickness and fears: our maimed and ambivalent sexuality, our terror of the idiot mass, our helpless empathy with suffering, our love perverted into sadism and masochism.

45

West did this in convincing present-day forms of the great myths: the Quest, the Scapegoat, the Holy Fool, the Dance of Death. His strength lay in his vulgarity and bad taste, his pessimism, his nastiness. West could never have been the affirmative political writer he sometimes imagined, or written the novels that he told his publisher, just before his death, he had planned: "simple, warm and kindly books." We must assume that if West had lived, he would have continued to write the sort of novels he had written before, perhaps even finer ones.

In his short tormented life, West achieved one authentically great novel, *Miss Lonelyhearts*, and three others less successful as wholes but full of brilliant and wonderful things. He was a true pioneer and culture hero, making it possible for the younger symbolists and fantasists who came after him, and who include our best writers, to do with relative ease what he did in defiance of the temper of his time, for so little reward, in isolation and in pain.

↙ Selected Bibliography

THE only book so far published on West is James F. Light's *Nathanael West: An Interpretative Study*, to which I am indebted for nearly all of my biographical information. All four of West's novels are available in the one-volume *The Complete Works of Nathanael West*. A West library thus consists essentially of two books.

Works of Nathanael West

The Dream Life of Balso Snell. Paris and New York: Contact Editions, 1931.
Miss Lonelyhearts. New York: Liveright, 1933.
A Cool Million. New York: Covici-Friede, 1934.
The Day of the Locust. New York: Random House, 1939.
"Some Notes on Violence," *Contact*, 1:132–33 (October 1932).
"Some Notes on Miss Lonelyhearts," *Contempo*, 3:1–2 (May 15, 1933).
"Business Deal," *Americana*, 1:14–15 (October 1933).
"Soft Soap for the Barber," *New Republic*, 81:23 (November 1934).

Current American Reprints

Miss Lonelyhearts. New York: Avon. $.25.
The Day of the Locust. New York: Bantam. $.25.
The Complete Works of Nathanael West. New York: Farrar, Straus, and Cudahy, 1957.

Bibliography

William White. "Nathanael West: A Bibliography," *Studies in Bibliography*, 11:207–24 (1958). (Papers of the Bibliographical Society of the University of Virginia, Charlottesville, Virginia.)

Critical and Biographical Studies

Aaron, Daniel. "The Truly Monstrous: A Note on Nathanael West," *Partisan Review*, 14:98–106 (February 1947).
————. "Writing for Apocalypse," *Hudson Review*, 3:634–36)Winter 1951(.
Coates, Robert M. "Messiah of the Lonely Hearts," *New Yorker*, 9:59 (April 15, 1933).

_____. Introduction to *Miss Lonelyhearts*. New York: New Directions, 1946, 1950.

Cohen, Arthur. "Nathanael West's Holy Fool," *Commonweal*, 64:276–78 (June 15, 1956).

Gehman, Richard B. Introduction to *The Day of the Locust*. New York: New Directions, 1950. (Reprinted in the Bantam edition.)

Liebling, A. J. "Shed a Tear for Mr. West," *New York World Telegram*, June 24, 1933, p. 14.

Light, James F. *Nathanael West: An Interpretative Study*. Evanston, Ill.: Northwestern University Press, 1961.

McKenney, Ruth. *Love Story*. New York: Harcourt, Brace and Company, 1950. Pp. 175–76, 195–97.

Podhoretz, Norman. "A Particular Kind of Joking," *New Yorker*, 33:156–65 (May 18, 1957).

Rosenfeld, Isaac. "Faulkner and Contemporaries," *Partisan Review*, 18:106–14 (January–February 1951).

Ross, Alan. Introduction to *The Complete Works of Nathanael West*.

Sanford, John. "Nathanael West," *Screen Writer*, 2:10–13 (December 1946).

Troy, William. "Four Newer Novelists," *Nation*, 136:672–73 (June 14, 1933).

Williams, William Carlos. "Sordid? Good God!" *Contempo*, 3:5, 8 (July 25, 1933).

_____. Review of *The Day of the Locust, Tomorrow*, 10:58–59 (November 1950).

Wilson, Edmund, "Postscript," *The Boys in the Back Room*. San Francisco: Colt Press, 1951.